This book belongs to...

_____

D0317474

Contents

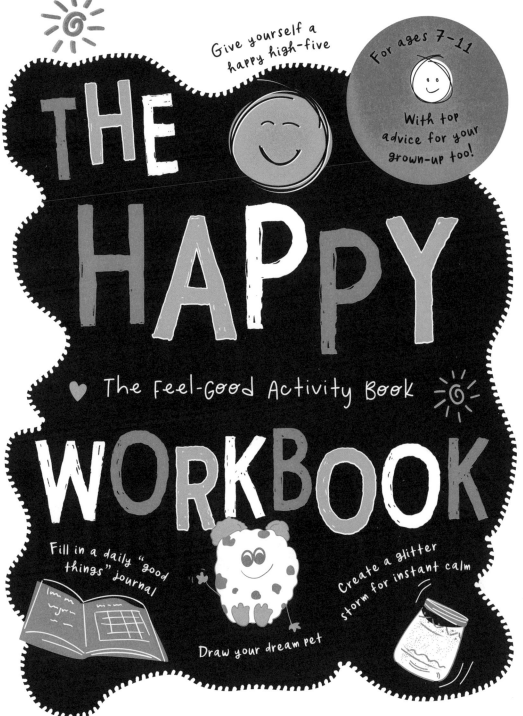

Give yourself a happy high-five

For ages 7–11

With top advice for your grown-up too!

THE HAPPY WORKBOOK

The Feel-Good Activity Book

Fill in a daily "good things" journal

Draw your dream pet

Create a glitter storm for instant calm

IMOGEN HARRISON

Foreword by **Amanda Ashman–Wymbs, BA (Hons) BACP accredited**

Substantial discounts on bulk quantities of Summersdale books are available to corporations, professional associations and other organizations. For details contact general enquiries: telephone: +44 (0) 1243 771107 or email: enquiries@summersdale.com.

FOREWORD

by Amanda Ashman–Wymbs BA (Hons) BACP accredited
(British Association for Counselling and Psychotherapy)

When children experience their natural happiness
becoming overshadowed with difficult feelings or
unhelpful thought patterns, they need to learn how to
get themselves back to a calm and content place within.

The Happy Workbook is a wonderfully supportive book,
full of fun activities and insights, which help children
to learn holistic and scientifically proven ways
of accessing inner happiness.

The easy-to-understand text and exercises encourage self-awareness, emotional understanding and the development of healthy self-esteem and self-confidence. Knowing and understanding how to stay happy is a great gift and resource to children now, and for the rest of their lives.

Welcome,
parents and carers!

Ask any parent or carer what they hope and dream for their child
as they are growing up and the answer is universal: "I want them to
be happy and feel loved." It sounds really simple, but the reality can
be much more challenging. We often think of happiness as just a
moment in time or a temporary experience, but lasting contentment is
much more complex. In a world where 10–20 per cent of children and
adolescents are experiencing mental health disorders – with half of all
mental illnesses beginning by the age of 14* – making sure our children
have a positive outlook on life has never been more important.

Your child's behaviour is a useful indicator of how they are feeling, particularly
in the case of younger children, who may not have the vocabulary to put their
feelings and emotions into words. If your child does seem unhappy, don't
panic! This book offers creative ways for your child to explore their feelings,
and will help them work through the reasons why they might be feeling this
way. The activities will show them how to build a positive sense of self and
outlook by looking at what makes them the unique and special people they
are, as well as offering ways to approach life's challenges with confidence.

You know your child best and it's up to you whether you choose to work with
them on the activities, but let them lead the conversation and be careful not
to influence their responses. Support them through active listening so that
your child feels safe expressing their feelings to you, and, when the time is
right, paraphrase what they have said to affirm and empathize with them.

Not every child will want to write down or discuss specific thoughts, and this is where the same themes in this book can be explored through activities that capture your child's imagination, such as using building blocks, singing or any other creative play. Research has found that expressing difficult emotions through play is one of the most effective ways for children to process their feelings and improve their mental health.

Look out for the parent/carer and child icons, as these are signposts for more technical information about the relevance and usefulness of a specific activity.

I hope this book is a fun and uplifting journey for you and your child. There is further content for parents and carers at the end of the book.

9

*Source: World Health Organization

HI THERE!

Being happy feels great. When we're happy we feel contented, energized and strong. That's because when we are enjoying ourselves our brains produce happy hormones that make us feel fantastic.

But sometimes it can be hard to feel happy. There are many reasons for this and it's different for everyone.

Here are some questions to ask yourself: Do you often...

- have sad thoughts in your head that you struggle to get rid of?

- feel unconfident about making new friends?

- feel annoyed when things don't go right?

- struggle with making decisions for fear that you will make the wrong one?

- find it hard to relax?

- worry about being away from your grown-up?

If you are nodding your head while reading this list, then you have come to the right place. The good news is that there are lots of things you can do to feel happy again and this book is here to show you how. With the help of some fun challenges and activities, including making paper boats, designing your dream pet and creating a happy poster you'll be able to turn your frown upside-down.

At the end of the book, you will have your own unique happy toolkit, a special list of things that work for you whenever you are feeling sad that will put a smile on your face and help you see the bright side.

Take your grown-up along for the ride, because there are special tips throughout for them to read with you if you want, and activities that could be fun to do together! Look for this icon for the special tips:

Let's get started...

TALKING ABOUT IT

Having someone to talk to when you're feeling unhappy can make you feel much better. They can help you find ways to feel more positive and see the good in things. On this page, write down your three most favourite grown-ups that you feel you can talk to about anything that's worrying you. Make sure you add big smiles to their faces too!

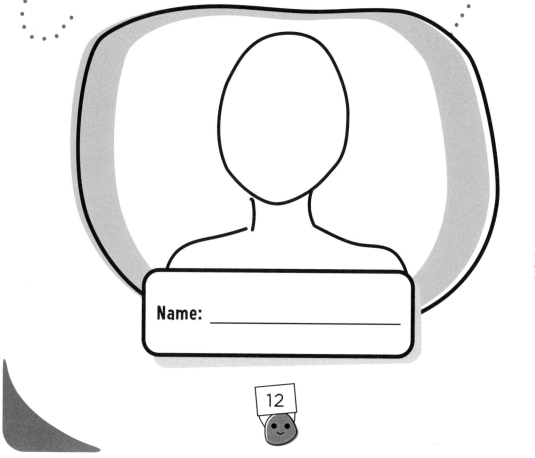

Name: _____

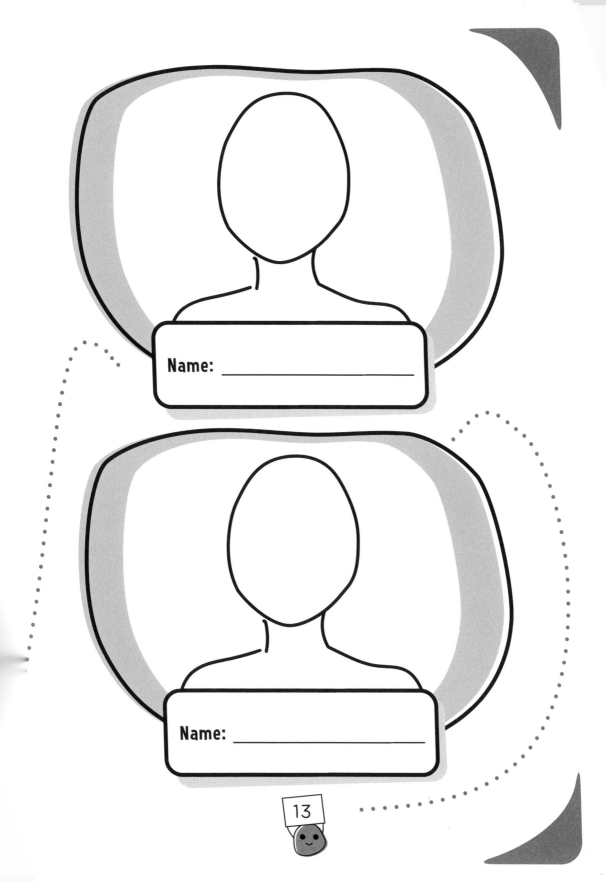

Name: _____

Name: _____

13

MY GALLERY OF HAPPY THINGS

Working out the things that make you happy is important
for when you need something to make you feel good.

What makes you happy? Fill in the frames using
the hints beside each to create a gallery of happy
things. You can write or draw the happy stuff.

My happy friends

My happy pets

My happy things to do

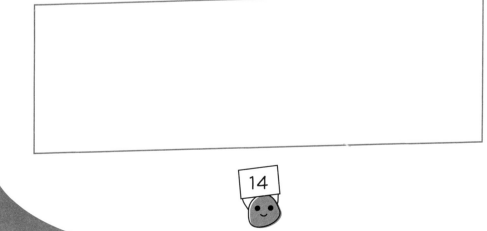

My happy games

My happy sounds

My happy food

When we write down the things that make us happy it helps us to feel good about ourselves and makes us feel stronger and better equipped to cope when we're upset. Make sure you return to this list as a reminder of the things that make you happy the next time you are feeling sad.

How are you feeling?

We feel lots of different emotions every day, and every single one of them is OK. Sometimes it's hard to name the emotions that we are feeling and that's OK too. Colour in the delicious ice cream with your favourite rainbow colours. It's a special type of ice cream because it will reveal all your moods when you have coloured it in!

First colour in the key below with all the colours of the rainbow.

16

17

INNER STRENGTH

Growing up is great, and every new day offers new challenges.
When we're feeling unhappy, though, we sometimes don't
want to try new things because we're worried that we
might not be good enough or look silly. Here's a great
exercise to help you see new challenges in a new way.
It involves looking at what you can do now compared
to a whole year ago. A year is a long time, after all!

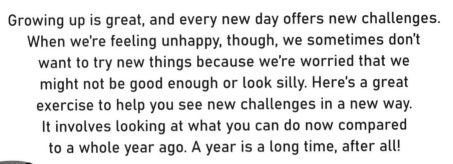

Last year I was _____ **years old**

Now, I am _____ **years old**

Think back over the past year and answer
the following questions: (You can write your
answers or talk about them with your
grown-up)

**What piece of schoolwork are you
particularly proud of?**

_____

_____

What's your special sporting skill?

_____

_____

How did you help a friend in need?

_____

What's the bravest thing you tried?

What's the funniest thing you have done to make a friend laugh?

What new skills have you learned?

What scary things did you try?

Who did you speak to for the first time?

Looking back at times when you have overcome challenges, tried something new or helped someone will help you to see that you are strong, brave and kind. Seeing these achievements and talking about them with your grown-up will show you how far you've come and how brilliant you are!

MAKING MISTAKES

Sometimes we feel sad about ourselves because we feel we've done something bad or made a mistake and these sad feelings can hang around like a bad smell!

Everyone makes mistakes – even grown-ups – and rather than feeling regret or wishing you could jump in a time machine and go back and do things differently there is a much better way of looking at mistakes.

The messy splodges on these pages look like mistakes, but can you make something new out of them?

Hmm, is this a butterfly?

20

reminds me
of a slug

Mistakes help us learn and grow,
and they can lead us to find much
better solutions to our problems.
The next time you make a mistake,
be kind to yourself and see it as
a stepping stone to learning how
to do something better.

21

Paper chain of greatness

This activity requires glue, paper and scissors, and you might find yourself humming a few Christmas tunes if you've made paper chains as decorations before!

This is a little different, as the links in this chain are to remind you of all the different things that make you great. Begin by cutting out strips of paper (approx. 5 cm x 20 cm (2 in. x 8 in.) or use the template strips over the page). Once you have the strips, write down something you're proud of on each strip. It could be anything that makes you feel good about yourself. Here are some prompts to start you off:

I made it on the team at school.

I helped my friend when they fell over.

I tidied my room.

24

I can count to ten in French.

I can draw an elephant.

When you have your strips, create the first link by taping the ends of one strip together to form a circle, making sure the writing is on the outside. Then loop the next strip through the first link and tape its ends, and so on, until you have a chain. The great thing is you can keep adding to it whenever you have done something new that makes you feel happy about yourself. Make sure you hang up your chain somewhere where you can see it every day and maybe even wear it on special occasions!

This fun exercise helps you to identify your amazing skills and abilities to help your self-esteem shine. It also helps you to appreciate the unique skills of other people, like those of your friends and family.

25

JUST SMILE!

Your face is amazing. Just think of all the facial expressions you can make – and that's because you have 43 muscles in your face! Let's exercise those muscles by trying some of these expressions – and make sure your grown-up does them too!

Wiggle your eyebrows one by one

Try to touch your nose with your tongue

Flare your nostrils

Wink the left eye, then the right

Pull the funniest face that you can manage.

Blow out your cheeks to make your face as round as possible.

Did you know?

You use 17 facial muscles when you smile, but you use all 43 of them when you frown!

Frown

Now, smile!

Even if you don't feel like smiling, turning up the corners of your mouth will boost your mood and trick your brain into feeling happier. This is because smiling releases endorphins, the body's natural feel-good chemicals. Scientists have discovered that the happy feelings you experience when you smile can reduce how much stress you feel and even help you to live longer!

Smiley faces

Draw smiles on all the creatures on this page.
They don't all need to be the same. Draw some
laughing and others just grinning broadly.

30

Seeing other people (or animals!) smile makes you happier too!

THE GOOD THINGS JOURNAL

When we're feeling sad, it can seem like every day is going to be a bad day. This is when you need to look extra hard for the good things. On these journal pages, write down three good things that happened each day over five days, and, if you can, the efforts that you made to make these things happen.

Day	Three good things	I made these things happen by...
Example	I made a new friend today.	I asked if I could sit with them at lunchtime and we told each other jokes.
	I tidied my room.	I put my magazines in a pile and organized my craft drawer.
	I did eight keepie-uppies in football practice.	I used my skills I'd learnt in class and kept practising.

Day	Three good things	I made these things happen by...

Day	Three good things	I made these things happen by...

36

Day	Three good things	I made these things happen by...

Keeping a good things journal is a great habit to get into, as it teaches us to reflect on positive experiences, which will help develop a happier outlook and build confidence and self-esteem — these are essential skills that will help you throughout your life. Good things aren't always about winning and being the best at something, but about the effort and hard work you have put in.

37

Learn to be an optimist

When you have a positive attitude, even when things seem to be going wrong, you see problems as temporary and feel confident you will overcome them. So how do we build a positive attitude and think like an optimist? This is a fun exercise to do with your family members. It's called Hero of the Day! The best time to do this is around the dinner table or any time when you're all in one space, such as on a car journey. Take turns to nominate a hero in the family and say why they deserve to be called a hero. Maybe you're your own hero for helping someone with jobs they had to do, or maybe your grown-up is your hero because they made you the tastiest lunch box. Anyone can nominate anyone else, even more than once!

According to scientists, children who have a positive attitude are happier than those who dwell on sad things or see life as difficult in general. Children who see things in a positive way tend to be more successful at school, are generally healthier and less likely to feel depressed.

Hero of the Day

41

POSITIVE SELF-TALK

Positive self-talk is when we talk kindly to ourselves in a reassuring and helpful way. For example, imagine you got the results of a school test and you didn't do as well as you'd hoped. It's easy to tell yourself off by saying you should have done better. A more reassuring and kinder thing to say to yourself would be something like, "I tried my best and it's OK to make mistakes. I will keep trying and will do better next time."

Here is a list of positive affirmations that you might like to say to yourself.

I deserve to be happy

I am my own superhero

I can do hard things

42

I forgive myself for my mistakes as they help me learn and grow

I am loved

I see so many good things in my life

I feel happy in myself

I am good enough

Take notice of the language of your thoughts and, next time you catch a negative one, try changing it to be positive. For instance, "This is too hard" or "I can't do this" could become "This is hard but I will try my best." Thoughts such as "I am helpless" or "There is nothing I can do" could become "I feel helpless, but I know that even small actions can make a difference" or "I will do whatever I can do."

Taking on a difficult challenge – one step at a time

We face new challenges every day, and some can seem so big that we want to run in the opposite direction to avoid them! The best thing to do to make a challenge less scary is to break it down into steps so you can build up the confidence to tackle it.

Look at the ladder on the opposite page to see how a big challenge can be broken down into simple steps. Now use the empty ladder and write the thing you find most challenging at the top. Next, think about what smaller steps you can take to reach your goal and write them on each step – ask your grown-up to help if you like.

Building up your confidence with each step will equip you with the positive mindset needed to tackle any challenge.

44

**Speak in front
of the class**

**Final
rehearsal the
night before**

**Practise in
front of your
family**

**Sing songs loudly
on the way to
school in the car**

**Practise in
front of your
grown-up**

**Read aloud
on your own**

45

HAPPY HIGH-FIVES

Draw around your hand on the blank page and write a compliment (something nice to say about yourself) on each finger and one in the palm, like in the example below.

I'm a good friend

I listen well in class

I can draw hedgehogs

I played with my sister

I am good at looking after my hamster

Saying and thinking nice things about yourself will give you a big confidence boost and a happier outlook. Say these compliments out loud every morning. It will set you up for a good day. You can draw a new Happy High-Five every day or every week — it's up to you.

Jar of compliments

Compliments are good for you and they make you feel really good about yourself. Here's a way to save up all the nice things that people have said to you. It could be about anything – your good manners, work you have done, a special skill, anything at all.

Write down a compliment every time you receive one on a slip of paper, then pop it in a jam jar, so when you need a little happiness boost, you can pick out a compliment, or a handful!

HOW TO MAKE YOUR COMPLIMENTS JAR

1. Get a clean jam jar or clear container (ask first!).

2. Place the jam jar upside down on a piece of paper and draw a circle that's a thumb-size bigger than the jar, all the way round.

3. Cut out the paper circle, then fold it in half and snip a letterbox-shaped hole in the middle.

48

4. Flatten the circle and place it on top of the opening of the jar, and squash the edges down the sides of the jar.

5. Get a rubber band and secure the paper over the top of the jar so it stays put.

6. Now you have your compliments jar, ready to fill with nice things people say to you!

7. Cut some strips of paper ready to write all the compliments down for posting into the jar.

8. You can decorate the jar with marker pens or glass pens or stick stickers on to personalize it.

When you want to take out the compliments, carefully remove the lid by pulling the elastic band.

Receiving a compliment can make your day. Be sure to thank someone when they have given you a compliment and take a moment to truly enjoy what has been said.

LETTING GO OF SAD FEELINGS

We all experience feelings of sadness, anger, hurt and worry. It's normal and it's OK. It's good to feel these feelings and then let them go, because it will make it easier to deal with these uncomfortable feelings the next time.

This activity will help you acknowledge your frustration, anger or sadness and will help you let it go.

Get a piece of paper and write down the thing that's upsetting you and how it's making you feel. For example, "I wasn't invited to a birthday party and it made me feel sad and lonely."

When you have finished writing, take the piece of paper and scrunch it up in as tight a ball as you can manage. Really squeeze it and rip it if you want to. Take out your frustrations on the piece of crumpled paper.

Once you've finished squashing the paper, it's time to get rid of it, by either throwing it in the recycling or compost heap, or burying it in the garden where it will disappear, along with your sad feelings.

PAPER BOATS

Other ways to let go include making a paper boat out of the piece of paper and watching it float away down a stream. Or, if you live near a lake or the sea, find some flat skimming stones, and paint your words on them before skimming them into the water and watching them disappear.

1
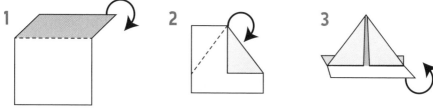

2
3

4
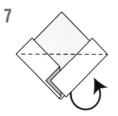

5
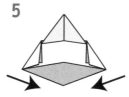

6
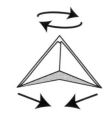

7
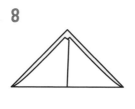

8

9

10
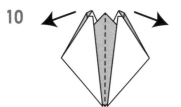

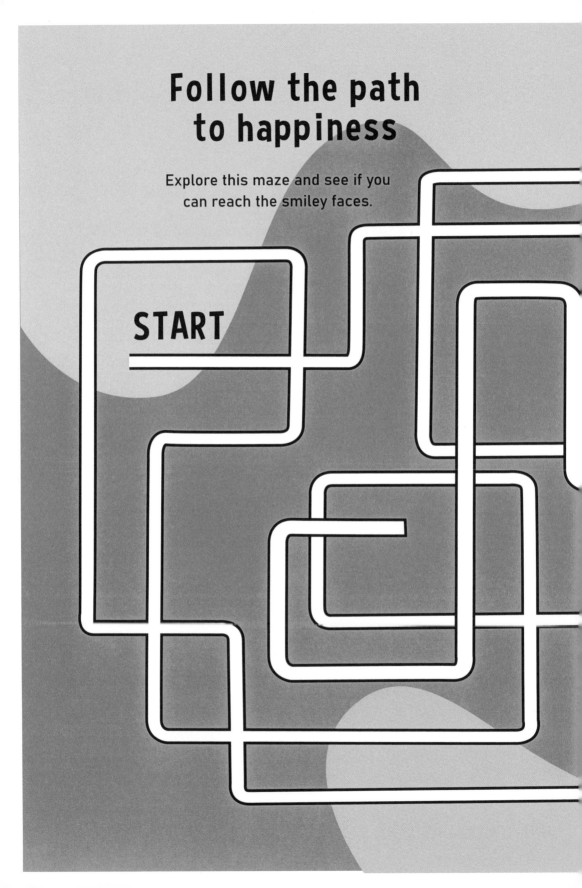

Follow the path to happiness

Explore this maze and see if you can reach the smiley faces.

START

Get moving!

When you're feeling down in the dumps, one of the best ways to boost your mood is to do some exercise. Once you get your heart rate thumping, your body will release feel-good endorphins, providing a welcome distraction to things that might be bothering you.

The best thing about exercise is that you don't need any special equipment. Try this mini-workout with your grown-up and see how you both feel afterwards. You could even time each other – the one who finishes first is the winner!

1. Do 20 hops on your left foot, then 20 with your right foot. If you lose your balance you have to start again!

2. Crouch down and imagine you're a little animal and do 20 circuits of the biggest room in your house. Be careful to move things that will break easily out of the way first!

3. Gallop like a horse on the spot and see who can do the best neigh! You might need someone else to judge who is best!

4. Use a step in your house and step up and down 20 times.

5. Squat down as if you're sitting on an invisible chair and see how long you can stay in this position.

6. Now, see who is the most ticklish!

Exercising with your grown-up is great because it means you can motivate each other and have fun at the same time. According to research, just 20 minutes of exercise can boost your mood for up to 12 hours. See if you can do 20 minutes every day and see how much happier you feel!

DANCE MOVES

Dancing is great fun and it's also a good workout. Get your dancing shoes on (or your slippers!) and have a boogie to some tunes on the radio or smart device. See if you can tell the story of a song with your body movements! Write down your tracklist on the record on the opposite page!

See the funny side

Laughter is very good for you. Just like smiling, it releases endorphins, which make you feel happy, but it's good for your health too! A good giggle is like exercising, because it gets your blood flowing and your muscles working. Scientists have even discovered that it reduces worry, improves your memory and can help you sleep better.

Did you know that the average child laughs 400 times a day? Why don't you challenge yourself to laugh even more times than this! Try answering some of these questions – you can write down your answers or talk about them with your grown-up and watch them split their sides with laughter too!

60

What's the funniest thing that happened to you or a friend at school?

_____

_____

_____

What's the funniest book you have ever read and why?

_____

_____

_____

Who makes you laugh the most and why?

_____

_____

_____

What's the funniest joke you have ever heard?

_____

_____

_____

_____

Now try this activity. Draw a picture of your grown-up laughing – see how many creases you can see around their eyes and make sure you add them to the picture!

Now, draw yourself laughing too!

Scientists who research brain functions have found that when you hear a person laugh, it triggers a region of your brain that makes you feel as though you are laughing too! Wow!

Just play!

Playing is good for you in so many ways – it helps you to use your imagination, to let off steam and have fun with friends.

Try out some of these things:

Have a treasure hunt around the house, as you look for everyday objects – see who can find the items the quickest.

Get your waterproofs and wellies on and splash about in the rain and the puddles.

Create an obstacle course in your living room – but make it safe with lots of cushions.

Play hide and seek.

Add some ideas of your own in the spaces below.

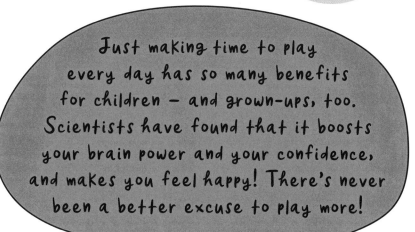

Just making time to play
every day has so many benefits
for children – and grown-ups, too.
Scientists have found that it boosts
your brain power and your confidence,
and makes you feel happy! There's never
been a better excuse to play more!

MINDFULNESS

We all have feelings of worry and sadness sometimes, but this isn't a bad thing – it's a sign that we are emotionally healthy – even though at the time it can feel uncomfortable in our head and body. When we are unhappy in our head it can be helpful to try some calming techniques, and some of the best ways involve mindfulness, because your mind needs to be exercised too, just the same as your body.

Mindfulness means giving your full attention to the present moment, slowing down and being calm. It sounds simple – and it is! Anyone can do it and it has so many magical benefits:

It can make you feel happier

It can make you feel more relaxed when faced with challenges

Helps you to manage and overcome difficult feelings

It helps you to listen and improves your memory

It's great for your self-esteem

Mindfulness is a fun thing to do with your grown-up and it's a skill that you can carry with you for your whole life! Try out some of the fun mindfulness exercises on the next few pages.

MINDFULNESS EXERCISE 1: MEDITATION

Boost your happiness levels by following the simple steps in this meditation with your grown-up.

1. **Sit somewhere comfortable and quiet and close your eyes.**

2. **Try to clear your mind of distractions and focus on your breathing, concentrating on each in and out breath.**

3. Tune into your body and how it feels, starting with the top of your head, then neck and shoulders, and gradually work your way down your body to the tips of your toes.

4. When you have finished, slowly open your eyes and enjoy the sense of calm that you feel.

People who practise regular meditation, like Buddhist monks, have been found to have happiness levels that are off the charts! If you practise mindfulness for just 10 minutes a day, you will be happier and more confident when it comes to handling upsets. There are apps available to try guided meditation, which can be a great way to relax and feel calm.

MINDFULNESS EXERCISE 2:
GLITTER STORM FOR INSTANT CALM

Who doesn't love glitter?! A glitter storm is like a snow globe but with glitter inside it. A glitter shaker can help you to feel calm instantly. Simply give it a shake and place it on a surface. Then take a moment to watch the glitter sparkle and gently fall and settle to the bottom of the jar. As the glitter settles, you will feel calmer again. Here's how to make one:

1. **Find a glass jar with a screw-top lid. Give it a clean in warm water.**

2. **Decorate the jar on the outside with tissue paper or glass paint, if you have it, and leave to dry.**

3. **Once dry, fill the jar with water, then add two dessert spoons of eco-friendly glitter – it can be any colour you like.**

4. Glue around the inner rim of the lid and screw it on top of the jar. Allow it to dry.

5. Your glitter jar is ready to use. Give it a shake and watch the glitter float and fall.

Keep your glitter jar in a safe place so you can use it whenever you are feeling worried or upset. Imagine all the specks of glitter are your individual thoughts whizzing around your brain, so that when they settle to the bottom of the jar, you feel more settled too.

MINDFULNESS EXERCISE 3:
DRAW YOUR EMOTIONS

It can be difficult to explain in words how you feel sometimes. That's where drawing can really help you to express your emotions.

Close your eyes for a moment and really think about how you are feeling. How does it feel in your body and in your mind? Then open your eyes. Now, on the blank page, draw your feelings. You don't need to draw a "thing", it could be lines or scribbles or dots – do whatever feels right to you. Talk with your grown-up about your drawing and see if any words spring to mind. Can you name your picture?

Try this activity at different times, whenever you are feeling strong emotions – not just sad or angry ones, they can be happy and joyful ones too!

MINDFULNESS EXERCISE 4:
FOUR SENSES

This is a super-simple exercise. The basic idea is to sit as still and as quietly as possible, and notice four things around you.

Start by finding a comfy place to sit with your grown-up.

Each of you takes it in turns to tell the other person something that they can:

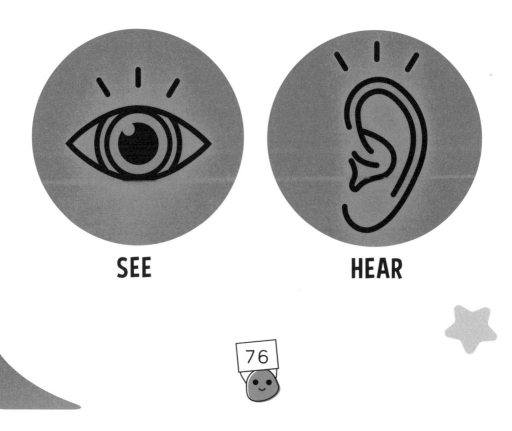

SEE   **HEAR**

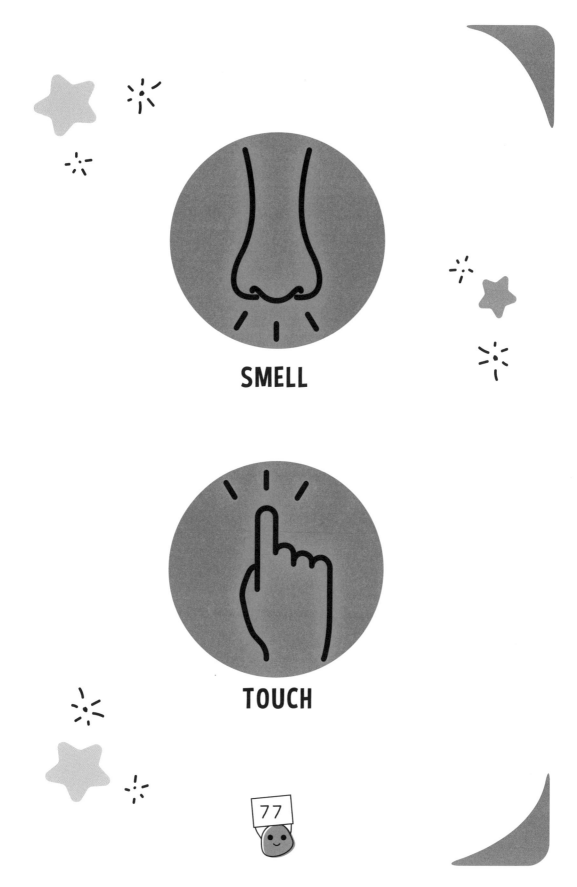

SMELL

TOUCH

77

Finding a happy place

Help the bear find his favourite tree by
following the bear tracks.

FINDING YOUR VOICE

Sometimes when we feel sad, it can make us not want to speak because we feel unconfident or embarrassed. The more we don't speak, the harder it becomes. Tongue twisters are used by everyone who needs to speak clearly and confidently; people like politicians, actors and teachers, or anyone giving a speech or trying to get their point across. Tongue twisters are like an exercise for your mouth to prepare it and you for speaking up and speaking out. Try these out to help you feel more confident about speaking up. It's also a really funny thing to do with your grown-up. See who can say them correctly and in the quickest time. Good luck!

Toy boat,
toy boat,
toy boat.
(say this 10
times fast)

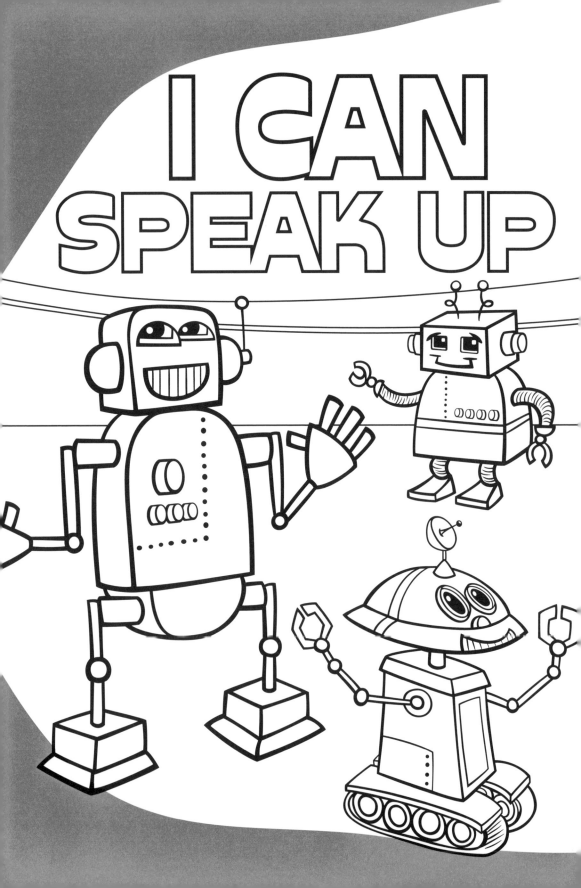

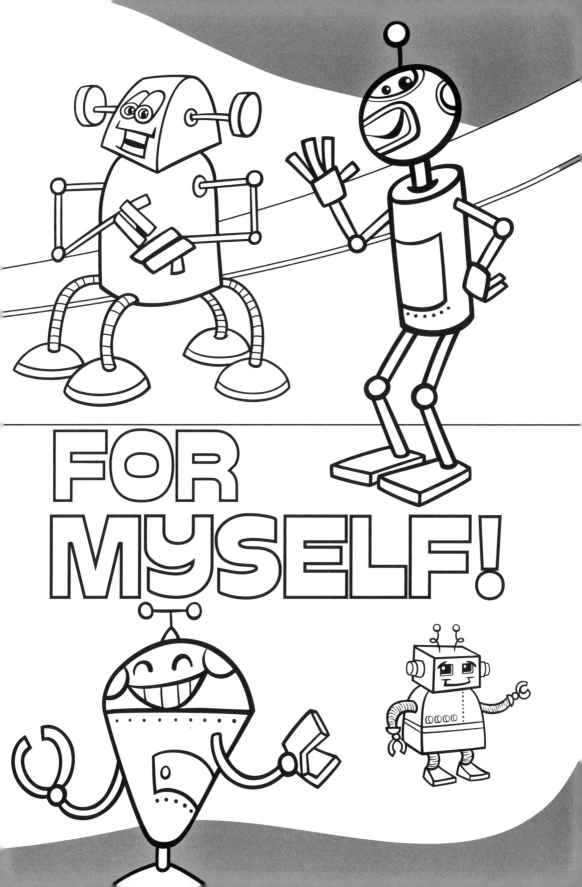

Good sleep = happy you

How much we sleep is linked to our happiness levels. When we don't have enough sleep, we are more likely to feel sad and grumpy. Sleep affects how well our brains work. When you have a tired brain you're more likely to feel bad-tempered, upset, sleepy and worried. When you have a well-rested brain after a good sleep, you feel refreshed, alert, confident and ready to take on the day.

Here are some tips for a better bedtime:

Try to get to bed at the same time every night, so you get the same amount of sleep.

Plan your own calming bedtime routine with your grown-up. It could involve a bubble bath, reading some of your favourite story or talking about your day over a warm drink.

Turn off screens at least an hour before bed, because the light from them can trick your brain into being wide awake. Instead, look at your Happy Gallery (page 14) or fill in the Good Things Journal (page 34).

The Sleep Council, which studies sleep habits and sleep quality, suggests that children between the ages 7–11 need 10–11 hours of sleep a night in order to function well the next day. Studies have shown that children who are well-rested have improved attention, behaviour, memory and happiness levels.

Create your happy place

Draw your dream den with your favourite things.
Imagine a space where you can go to feel calm and happy.
Add your favourite toys and books, pictures of your
favourite people and places, a squishy cushion to sit on,
and your favourite colours on the wall.

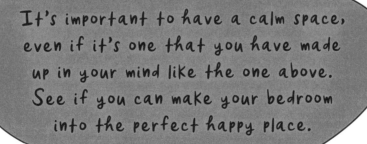

It's important to have a calm space, even if it's one that you have made up in your mind like the one above. See if you can make your bedroom into the perfect happy place.

87

BEDTIME STORIES

Stories are a magical way to disappear into new worlds and have adventures. Reading stories sparks your imagination. Scientists have found that people who read stories are generally happier as it exercises the mind in the same way as active positive thinking.

Write the titles of your favourite books on the spines below.

According to research, reading before bedtime helps to reduce your worry levels by 70 per cent!

Small acts of kindness

Being kind and showing kindness to others is a lovely thing to do, and it makes you feel good too! Here are some ideas for things that you can do to spread kindness:

SENDING KIND MESSAGES

Everyone likes to receive messages of support and kindness. Have a think about the people in your family or your friends at school. Write down the names of your three favourite people on the notes below, then write a nice message to each of them. It could be to thank them for being there for you when you needed them, or for being a good friend.

Name:
Message:

Name:
Message:

Name:
Message:

SMILE AND THE WORLD SMILES BACK

Get in the habit of smiling at the people you know when you see them out and about or in school. It's very likely that the people you smile at will smile back, and they in turn will smile at others too.

RANDOM ACTS OF KINDNESS

Think of ways you could do something nice for someone else. It could be as simple as helping to carry something, or helping them to look for something. The more kind things that you do for others, the more others will do kind things for you!

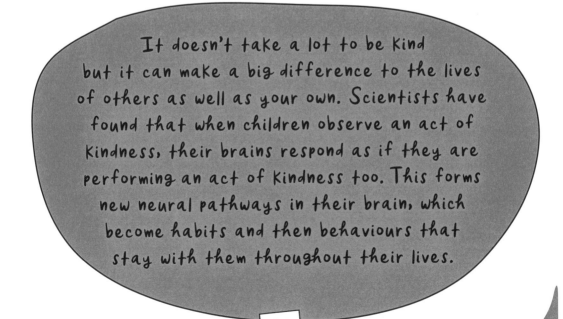

It doesn't take a lot to be kind but it can make a big difference to the lives of others as well as your own. Scientists have found that when children observe an act of kindness, their brains respond as if they are performing an act of kindness too. This forms new neural pathways in their brain, which become habits and then behaviours that stay with them throughout their lives.

IN THEIR SHOES

If we want to understand people better, we need to imagine being in their shoes. This doesn't mean taking their shoes off their feet and putting them on ours – although that would be quite funny! – it means imagining what they're feeling and why they might be feeling this way. This is called empathy. Empathy is very important as it helps us to be kinder and happier people.

Here are some faces with different expressions. Can you match the expressions to the emotions listed down the middle?

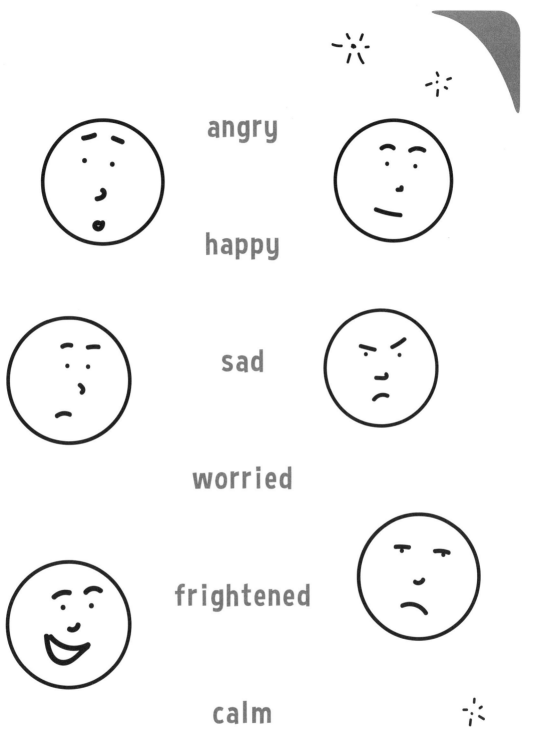

angry

happy

sad

worried

frightened

calm

Spending time with friends

Having friends is good for your self-esteem and confidence, which means it's good for your happiness levels too! Fill in the questions below about your best friend.

Who is your best friend?

_____

What games do you like to play together?

_____

When and where did you become friends?

_____

What makes them a good friend?

_____

What makes you a good friend?

_____

Three words that best describe your friend:

_____

Three words that best describe you as a friend:

_____

Best indoor games you play together:

_____

Best outdoor games you play together:

_____

Happy poster

Create a happy poster with some happy
words and pictures. You will need a large piece
of paper or card and some old magazines
or catalogues (ask a grown-up first!).

Cut out images from the magazines that make you
happy – it could be a picture of a puppy, or a delicious
cake, or a treehouse – anything that makes you smile.

Write HAPPY in the middle of the paper, then
decorate the space around it by gluing the cut-out
images of all the things that make you feel happy.

Hang it somewhere where you'll see it every day,
like on your bedroom door or on the fridge.

Happy   Happy

HAPPY

Happy

Happy   Happy

Happy

99

MY DREAM PET

Pets can be wonderful for your happiness and they have been found to make you feel calmer and less worried. Pets provide a sense of belonging and teach responsibility and kindness. This activity is for you, whether you have a pet or not. It's time to design your dream pet. Start by answering the questions below to help you decide what sort of pet your dream pet might be.

What do they eat?

Do they have fur, feathers or fins?

Are they cuddly?

What sort of noise do they make?

Can they fit in your pocket?

Are they bigger than you?

Do they need to go for walkies?

What will you name them?

What colour are they?

Now draw your dream pet on the opposite page.

Get outside in nature

Most people don't need an excuse to spend time outside, because being in nature is fun and is a brilliant mood booster.

Try some of these nature activites with your grown-up.

Have a walk in the woods.

Build a den in the garden or the woods for a forest fairy or goblin with twigs and leaves found on the ground.

Collect as many different leaves as you can find and identify them when you get home.

Make a tiny door for a tree elf.

Listen to birdsong and see how many different calls you can hear.

Go fruit picking.

Climb a hill and admire the view from the top.

Enjoy a picnic on the beach.

Many studies have shown that children who spend time outdoors in nature are happier, smarter, more focussed at school and less stressed than those that don't.

PROBLEMS CAN BE FUN!

They really can! Finding solutions to problems gets you thinking creatively. It makes you think like an engineer as you identify a problem, brainstorm solutions, make a plan and try it out.

Try to find solutions to these problems. Remember to make a plan first and then try it out. Good luck!

Can you build a house using only twigs, leaves and sticky tape?

Can you turn some foil and paperclips into a piece of jewellery?

Can you make a construction block tower that's taller than you?

Can you turn a ball of wool into a spider's web as big as your bedroom?

Can you get across your room without touching the wool?

Problem solving encourages you to see that life is full of multiple solutions and opportunities, all of them unique. Wondering "what could be" is fundamental – not just because it is an aptitude required at school, but because it helps us to realize our dreams and ambitions.

PROBLEM-SOLVING PLAN

The next time you're facing a problem, however big or small, try filling in the chart below to help you make a plan before you try it out!

The problem I'm facing is:

Different ways I can solve my problem:

1 ☆

2 ☆

3 ☆

Think about what would happen for each of the solutions you wrote above.

Colour in the star next to the solutions you will try!

The problem I'm facing is:

_____

_____

Different ways I can solve my problem:

1 _____ ☆

2 _____ ☆

3 _____ ☆

Think about what would happen for each of the solutions you wrote above.

Colour in the star next to the solutions you will try!

A recipe for happiness

This book is full of ideas of ways to make you happy! Now you've done some of them, you should have some great ideas for what helps you to feel happier. This is your recipe for happiness. Ask your grown-up to help you decide on the ingredients and write them on the recipe page below. The ingredients are all the things that make you happy, so it could be anything from being in nature to hopping on one leg. Now, imagine the recipe made the most delicious food and draw it on the plate on the next page.

Ingredients

_____

_____

_____

_____

_____

_____

_____

Method

_____

_____

_____

_____

_____

_____

_____

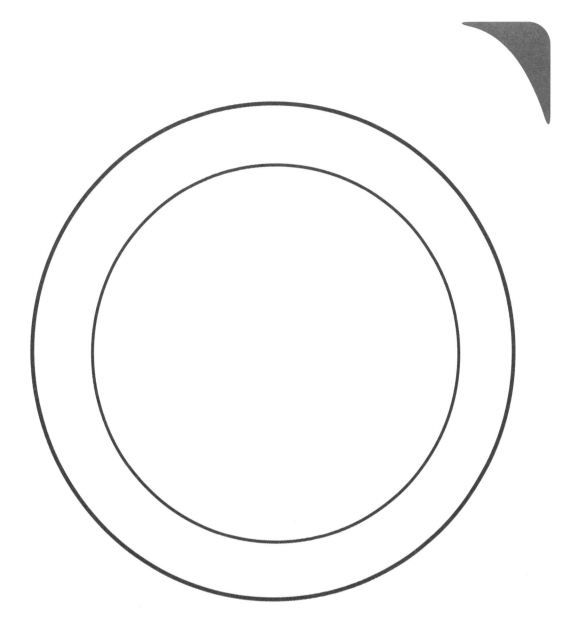

Yum, that looks delicious!

Mood tracker

Tracking your moods can be useful, as it can help to see if there are any particular times when you are feeling low and to work out why this might be. Fill in the mood tracker over the following pages. Draw in a face with the expression that best describes your mood each day for a whole month.

Mon	Tues	Wed	Thurs	Fri	Sat	Sun

KEY

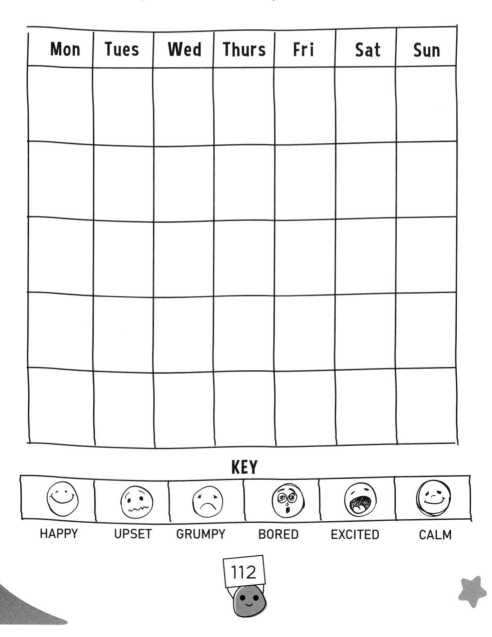

| HAPPY | UPSET | GRUMPY | BORED | EXCITED | CALM |

Mon	Tues	Wed	Thurs	Fri	Sat	Sun

KEY

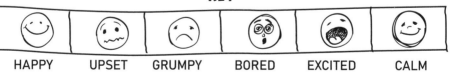

HAPPY	UPSET	GRUMPY	BORED	EXCITED	CALM

Mon	Tues	Wed	Thurs	Fri	Sat	Sun

KEY

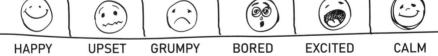

HAPPY	UPSET	GRUMPY	BORED	EXCITED	CALM

Mon	Tues	Wed	Thurs	Fri	Sat	Sun

KEY

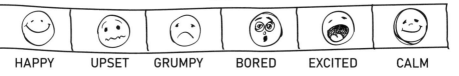

HAPPY	UPSET	GRUMPY	BORED	EXCITED	CALM

115

Conclusion

Hopefully the skills you have learned in this book should go a long way to helping you feel more positive and see life as one of exciting opportunities and new experiences. We all deserve to feel happy, and knowing that you can calm yourself when you are worried, find solutions to difficulties by making a plan and trying it out, or simply smiling to convince your brain into feeling good are skills that will be useful for your whole life, and don't forget, the more you practise these things, the happier you will be! You are brilliant!

Colour in, then cut out and keep these medals as a reminder of how great you are!

119

Mind your fingers ☺

Answers

Pages 54-55
Follow the path to happiness

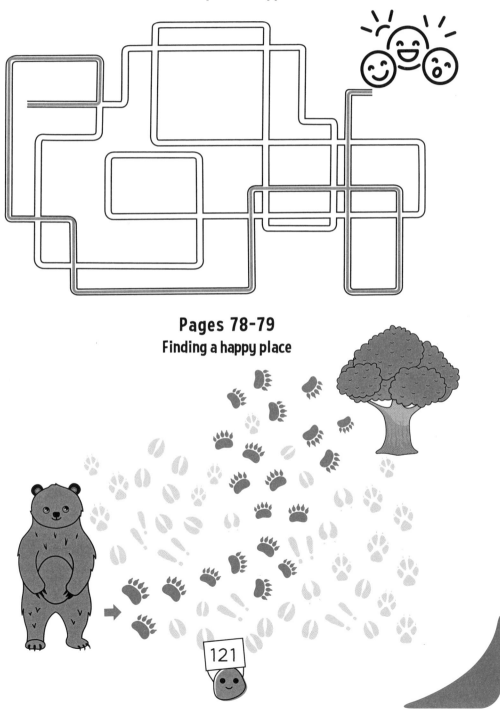

Pages 78-79
Finding a happy place

121

Final thoughts for parents and carers

I hope the activities in this book have been fun and inspiring, and your child can use their new-found skills to stay positive.

Happiness varies from person to person, and there is no one-size-fits-all solution to regulating moods because every human mind is different.

Here are some final thoughts to consider:

· Keep talking to your child and talk through their feelings, both good and bad. This way they will find it easier to deal with normal levels of low mood or difficult experiences when they arise, and know how to recognize and ask for help if they feel overwhelmed.

- If you feel that your child's low mood is having a negative effect on their daily life, it could be a good time to seek support outside the family. Start by talking to your child's school teacher or doctor. They'll be able to advise the next steps. Alternatively, you could go directly to a therapist to discuss your concerns. Involve your child in decision-making, listen to any concerns they have, validate and reassure them. Treat it just as you would if you were seeking for a physical health symptom. Remember: seeking support is a sign of strength and love, and you should never feel guilt or shame for doing so.

- When your child is struggling with their feelings, it can take a lot out of you. Make sure you have plenty of support too. It can be hard to ask for help initially, but just know that those who care about you will want to help and be there for you.

Keep going – you're doing great!

123

NOTES

NOTES

The Worry Workbook

Imogen Harrison

£10.99

Paperback

ISBN: 978-1-78783-537-5

Worries come in all shapes and sizes and can creep up on us when we least expect them. They are like little clouds that float above our heads that seem at once menacing and threatening, stopping us from doing the things we really want and spoiling our fun. *The Worry Workbook* is here to help by explaining what worry is, offering creative ways to calm and distract yourself when worry strikes.

- Make a worry camera that captures fears and shrinks them into a manageable size.
- Colour in a mood tracker that explores the rainbow of everyday emotions.
- Write on the magic mirror of compliments to help recognize your strengths.
- Create your very own list of anti-worry actions to fight fear and keep smiling.

This book has been peer reviewed by a child psychologist, and there are explainers throughout just in case your child has questions about the activities.